WILD FLOWERS OF THE BAILIWICK OF GUERNSEY

including Alderney, Sark and Herm
A Coloured Guide
edited by
Griff Caldwell

1994
published by La Société Guernesiaise
Candie Gardens, St Peter Port, Guernsey, GY1 1UG

First published 1994

Made and printed in Great Britain by
The Guernsey Press Co. Ltd, Guernsey, Channel Islands.

ISBN 0 9518075 3 6

TABLE OF CONTENTS

INTRODUCTION

This book has been written primarily for non-botanists, that is for those people who enjoy seeing wild-flowers and who wish to know a little more about what they are looking at. It is hoped that it will also be useful for children who are just becoming interested in wild-flowers. Those who find themselves enthused and interested in the whole subject of wild-flowers and plants can of course take their interest further by buying books which examine the subject more deeply. A list of reference books is on page 39.

The Bailiwick of Guernsey comprises the four main islands of Guernsey, Alderney, Sark and Herm. There are also four smaller islands, Lihou off the west coast of Guernsey and accessible at low tide, Brecqhou off the coast of Sark which is privately owned, Burhou off the coast of Alderney which is very difficult to visit and Jethou off the coast of Herm which is also privately owned.

Because the islands lie off the coast of Normandy nearly 100 miles south of the English coast they are relatively frost free. In addition of course being islands with a long seafaring tradition, particularly in Guernsey, many plants have been introduced into the islands either accidentally or on occasions on purpose. The result is that they support a very much wider range of plants than can normally be found in a comparable area in the United Kingdom or even in France nearby.

To enable the beginner, whether adult or child, to recognise and name the principal wild-flowers which he or she is likely to see when walking on the cliffs, on the low coast or through the lanes of the island, approximately 160 of the better known flowering plants have been selected. They have been divided into a number of groups corresponding with the habitats in which they are most likely to be found. This is to help with identification. Naturally many of the plants are found in more than one habitat. The habitat in which they have been grouped is the one in which they are most likely to be found.

It will also be noted that against the notes on each plant there is an indication that the plant can also be found or not found in Alderney, Sark or Herm. A + against A, S or H means that it can be found in Alderney, Sark or Herm. A - means that it cannot be found there.

To make things easier, particularly for the visitor, maps of all four islands have been provided showing in broad terms the location of the various habitats together with a brief description of each island. This is to help people find some of the best places for seeing wild-flowers on the various islands. To avoid confusion it is probably best to use these habitat maps in conjunction with local maps showing roads, tracks and place names.

The coloured plates have been painted by Wendy Bramall, a well known botanical illustrator. She was born and educated in Guernsey and is a member of La Société Guernesiaise. The text has been edited by me, Griff Caldwell. I am not a trained botanist, although interested in wild-flowers. I hope that being a layman as it were, I have edited the book in such a way as to make it both intelligible and easy to use by beginners. Naturally I am much indebted to a number of other people for their contributions. In particular I would like to thank Brian Bonnard from Alderney, Marcia Marsden from Sark, Rachel Rabey who wrote the piece on Herm and Patience Ryan who not only wrote the piece on Guernsey but also helped with the whole book. I would like to thank Bridget Ozanne, Secretary of La Société's Botany Section, who has also been a great help with the whole book. Lastly many thanks to David McClintock, the author of the definitive work on the Wild Flowers of Guernsey, who has taken a great interest in the project.

The type setting and preparation of the maps was done by Barry Wells of Perry's in Guernsey assisted by Joan Bagley. They are both members of La Société. My wife Betty has done the original typing and I am very grateful to her.

HOW TO USE THE BOOK

The wild-flowers illustrated and described in this book are a selection of the more common flowers to be seen in the four islands. The descriptions which follow have been kept simple and not written in botanical terms so that beginners should not find them too difficult to understand.

The flowers have been grouped in the habitats where they are most likely to occur. These are the same as the groups in the illustrations. The order in which they are described in their various habitats corresponds to the order in the illustrations. For example the first plant illustrated on the plates under 'Cliffs and Cliff Valleys' will also be the first plant described under Cliffs and Cliff Valleys in the text. However please remember that whilst many plants can only be found in quite specific habitats, others are very common and are often found in many different habitats. If, therefore, you do not find a flower illustrated in one habitat do not give up but try to find it in another one.

If you are completely stuck please ring La Société Guernesiaise on 725093. They will put you in touch with one of a number of botanists in the islands who will do their best to help you.

HABITATS

INTRODUCTION

Gardeners will know for example that some plants such as rhododendrons will only do well on an acid soil while others will only do well on alkaline soil. Similarly some plants such as Flag Iris will only do well in damp areas while others like it dry. What we are starting to do when we describe land in these terms is to describe habitat or where specific plants and indeed many types of animals such as birds or insects do best.

An indication as to which habitat a plant is likely to be found in is often a help in identifying it. Thus you would be unlikely to find Ragged Robin on a dry common or cliff. Similarly you would not find Sea Campion, a typical cliff plant, in a wet meadow.

It is for this reason that the plants illustrated in this book have been grouped into the habitats which have been described below. However do not be upset or put off if you find a wild flower in a habitat under which it is not illustrated Some plants are very adaptable and can be found in more than one habitat. A good example of this is the primrose which will be found in most of the habitats described here.

CLIFFS

All the islands have fairly extensive cliff habitats, mainly on the south coasts but all the way round in Sark. As they are south facing, they receive sun all day but are very exposed to the elements. The highest cliffs reach about 80-90 m.

Short rabbit grazed turf occurs at the top of most cliffs, supporting many of the same small flowers seen on the common e.g. Sand Crocus, Wild Thyme and Lady's Bedstraw. In spring (April and May) this area is often a blaze of colour with sheets of Sea Campion, Thrift, Bluebells and Common Bird's-foot Trefoil.

Below on the sheer rock faces only a few hardy species are able to survive. These are often succulent plants tolerant to salt spray.

CLIFF VALLEYS

The high cliffs to the south of Guernsey are folded in such a way that several damp valleys are formed. These have a characteristic flora of their own. As streams run down the bottom of the valleys to the sea many water-loving plants are found here such as Tufted Forget-me-not, Water Mint and Golden saxifrage. There are a few similar areas in Sark, one or two small damp valleys in Alderney but nothing quite the same in Herm.

COASTS AND COMMONS

Owing to their small size, all the islands come under a maritime influence. However the plants in this section are those most often seen on and around beaches and on the sandy land surrounding the coastal roads and paths.

There are now only small areas of sand dune in Guernsey and Alderney, none in Sark and rather more in Herm. These support a specialised flora of plants that are able to survive and grow where sands may be shifting and unstable. Certain plants such as Marram and Sand Sedge are very important as their roots bind and stabilize dunes.

Obviously coastal and cliff plants overlap to a great extent, although some plants grow exclusively in each habitat.

Fairly large areas of 'common' land exist in the north of Guernsey, Herm and Sark and the north east of Alderney. Many of the interesting plants in this habitat are very small and can only grow in the fine short turf which is produced by lack of moisture and grazing by rabbits.

WALLS AND BANKS

There are miles of walls and banks in the islands, enclosing the small fields and lining the lanes.

The flora of the solid high hedge banks varies according to how their owners treat them. All vegetation bordering the roads has, by law, to be cut twice a year so this also determines their character. Those that are cut very short will support smaller plants like Primroses, Violets and Barren Strawberry, whereas banks with more vigorous grasses may support Bluebells, Red Campion and Vetches. In May many roadside banks have a border of Stinking Onions.

Old walls often support many interesting plants. These are often garden escapes or alien and can best be seen in St Peter Port, where they probably originated, but they have now spread outwards to many areas. These include Red Valerian, Purple Toadflax, Ivy-leaved Toadflax and St Peter Port Daisy.

WET MEADOWS

Marshland and wet meadows are becoming increasingly rare in Guernsey due to drainage and drought. Luckily some of these low lying fields are conserved and managed by sympathetic private groups of individuals. This ensures the protection of some of our rarest and loveliest species. All the Orchids to be found in Guernsey are listed here in small areas, where they are quite abundant. The smaller islands have even less wetland areas. Many species listed here are not found in Herm at all. If not carefully managed the larger vigorous plants such as Hemlock Water Dropwort and Reed will take over and swamp Orchids and other smaller plants.

WASTELAND, GARDENS AND FARMLAND

Various areas are included in this section, such as derelict glasshouse sites, land around quarries, arable fields etc. The plants pictured are mainly those thought of as 'weeds' e.g. Common Ragwort and Black Nightshade. Others are really garden plants which seed themselves readily e.g. Giant Echium or are remnants of cultivation e.g. Gladiolus.

Many of these plants are likely to turn up when ground has been disturbed as their seeds can survive in the soil for many years until conditions are right for germination.

GUERNSEY

Guernsey slopes gently down from the steep south cliffs to the sandy dunes in the west and north. Inland the island is a network of roads and lanes, their walls and tree topped banks bright with wild flowers, among which can be seen Red Campion, Sheeps-bit and Alexanders thought to have been brought to England by the Romans for culinary purposes.

There are also a number of quiet narrow unsurfaced lanes known as 'Green Lanes', their sheltered banks a mass of ferns and flowers. In some of the south coast valleys are 'Water Lanes' where moisture-loving plants are found.

Flowers can be seen at almost any time of the year. Guernsey Coltsfoot,whose scented blooms are out in December and January is soon to be followed by Celandines , Violets and Primroses on lane side banks. But spring and early summer are the best times, when the Gorse on the cliffs is a mass of yellow blossom. The grassy slopes are carpeted by a profusion of flowers of many colours, and a relic of cultivation are the golden Daffodils.

The steep cliffs south of St Peter Port are covered with trees; in many places at their feet are Bluebells mixed with Red Campion and Stinking Onions, which with its white flowers looks like a white bluebell.

The west coast has a great deal to offer in the way of habitats, from small salty areas, shingle banks and wasteland to short sandy turf. Alien plants have established themselves in many of these habitats, and many seem to prefer waste places, so botanising offers endless pleasure. From South America came Cock's-eggs, Guernsey Fleabane and Fragrant Evening Primrose. The Tree Lupin is well established on some sand dunes. From South Africa we have Cape Cudweed and Kaffir-fig.

Several members of the onion family flourish here, including Wild Leek, Rosy Garlic and Neapolitan Garlic. Small-Flowered Melilot, Tree-mallow, Red Valerian and Gladiolus are all from the Mediterranean. The Duke of Argyll's Tea Tree originated in China. Plants have escaped from gardens and Giant Echium from the Canaries is one of these.

On the short sandy turf at L'Ancresse a whole collection of delightful miniature flowers can be found, but this also may mean going down on hands and knees.

A few wet meadows still survive where moisture-loving plants like Yellow Iris and Ragged Robin mingle with a variety of exotic Orchids. Walls abound in Guernsey, lining roads and lanes, propping up banks and holding St Peter Port together, where the charming St Peter Port Daisy is most abundant and from where it was first recorded in the British Isles. This is only a very brief introduction to the pleasures of looking for flowers in Guernsey.

GUERNSEY

1km

Cliffs

Coast and Common

Wetlands

Wet Valleys

L'Ancresse Common

Fort Doyle

Omptolle

Houmet Paradis

Grandes Rocques

St. Sampson

Cobo Bay

Vazon Bay

Lihou Island

Lihoumel

Talbot Valley

Fauxquet Valley

St. Peter Port

Les Hanois Lighthouse

Silbe Nature Reserve

Fermain

Pleinmont

St. Martin's Point

Petit Bôt

Moulin Huet

Jerbourg

Corbiere

La Moye

Icart

Peastacks

ALDERNEY

Alderney is a small island, 3.5 miles long x 1.5 miles at its widest point. It is characterised by a high plateau at about 280' over the whole of the south and west sides, with steep cliff-tops and many small, almost inaccessible bays. The area close to the cliff-tops is largely covered with gorse, bracken and bramble, with an area of heathland towards the west, and was formerly common land used for furze-cutting and rough grazing. Inland from this, the principal agricultural land of the Island, known as The Blayes, was still strip-farmed on the open field system until the Second World War. The soil is generally slightly acid, and a large part of the western end is now occupied by the airport.

The few wooded valleys are mostly on the north facing slopes either side of St. Anne, with Val du Sud (a corruption of 'Saule' meaning 'Willow') and Val Fontaine on the southern side. The area across the narrow waist of the island from Braye Bay to Longis Bay, including most of the golf course is one large dune area.

Platte Saline, the site of salt flats and the conger drying and salting area in Elizabethan times, is also a sand-dune area, formerly with a large pond at its western side at the end of the Mill-Stream. This has almost completely dried up in the last five years, due to the extraction of most of the water from above the former watermill for domestic purposes. The beach is of fine shingle.

Alderney has no salt-marsh areas, few marshy areas of more than a few dozen square metres, no rivers, and the only open areas of fresh-water still to be found are in man-made quarries. It therefore has a limited number of natural habitats. This fact, the frequent exposure to strong salt-laden winds right across the island, and the large population of rabbits, present for many centuries, have between them limited the type, and numbers of species of plant which may be found. Frosts and snow are rare and Alderney generally has about 100-150mm less rain a year than Guernsey, and about 100 hours less sunshine.

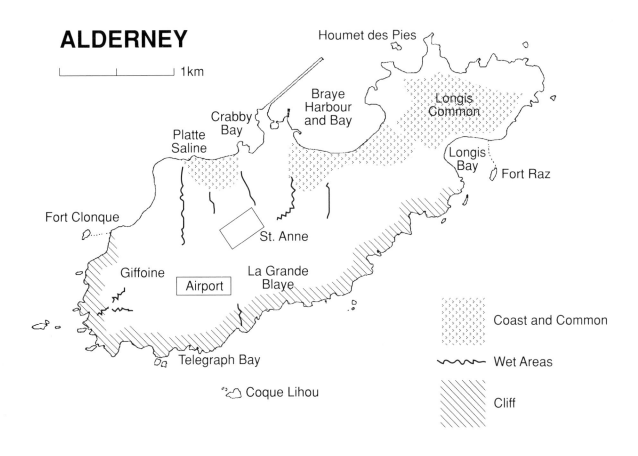

ALDERNEY

├──────────┤ 1km

Houmet des Pies

Braye Harbour and Bay

Crabby Bay

Longis Common

Platte Saline

Longis Bay

Fort Raz

Fort Clonque

St. Anne

Giffoine

La Grande Blaye

Airport

Telegraph Bay

Coque Lihou

Coast and Common

Wet Areas

Cliff

SARK

Sark is different from Guernsey as almost the whole coastline consists of cliffs. It is also different because the lack of modern intensive farming has left the majority of the fields unspoilt and much the way they have always been.

On a fine day the sea approaches to Sark give a good view of the cliffs. In spring these are covered with Bluebells, Thrift and Sea Campion. As you walk up Harbour Hill you will see Ox-eye Daisy and Stinking Onions, and if you take the footpath up through the wood you will find the curious spiky Butcher's Broom. Later in the year Ivy Broomrape grows beside the road.

At the top of the hill there are choices to be made, and if you hire a cycle you will be able to travel further and see more. Sark is much smaller than Guernsey and you will find its flowers distributed rather differently. Flowers of cliff and heathland are mostly to be found at opposite corners of the island; in the north on the Eperquerie Common, in the west on the area above Havre Gosselin and near the Pilcher Monument, and in the south above the south-west coast of Little Sark. Here in their seasons may be seen Sand Crocus, Gorse, Broom, Early Forget-me-not, Bell Heather, Lousewort and Autumn Squill. The spectacular causeway at La Coupée will show you Hare's-foot Clover, Kidney Vetch and Fennel. Not far away on the cliffs on either side are colonies of Burnet Rose which fill the June air with their spicy scent.

If shelter from the wind is needed, it is worth exploring wooded valleys above Port du Moulin or Greve de la Ville. Best of all is the Dixcart Valley where can be found Barren Strawberry, Hedge Woundwort and Gladdon.

Field paths lead past cultivated upland areas which still bear some arable weeds which are now becoming hard to find - Corn Marigold, Pale Flax and Small-flowered Catchfly among them. On cliff paths you will see Red Campion, Foxgloves, Lady's Bedstraw (yellow) and Hedge Bedstraw (white), Tormentil and its close relative Creeping Cinquefoil. Above Derrible Bay there is a fine colony of Violets, and Primroses are everywhere in quantity during the early spring.

Open valleys with water are few but repay a visit. Here may be found Yellow Iris, Yellow Bartsia, Heath Spotted Orchid and Lesser Spearwort. Nor should roadsides and verges be overlooked. Near gardens it is possible to find garden escapes such as Giant Echium, Tree Lupin and Tree Mallow. In the Churchyard and on lawns in neighbouring gardens spikes of Autumn Lady's-tresses appear in late summer when no mowing is needed.

It is hoped that the flowers in Sark will provide interest and pleasure - and perhaps a few surprises too.

SARK

├───────┤ 1km

Eperquerie
Landing

Port du Moulin

Greve
de la Ville

La Seigneurie

BRECQOU

La Maseline

Havre Gosselin

Harbour
Hill

Dixcart
Hotel

Derrible
Bay

Port es Saies

La Coupee

LITTLE
SARK

Coast and Common

Wet Valleys

HERM

A trip to Herm is a must and a walk round the island a delight. The boat leaves from St Peter Port and arrives in Herm at the harbour if the tide is high or at Rosaire Steps if it is low.

Having come ashore in Herm turn north and walk along the coastal path towards the common. When past the buildings you will see on your left Wild Leek with its onion flowers on long stalks, rare here but now spreading.

Reed grows right down to the beach. Soon you will pass under an archway of trees, mostly elm. Notice how the prevailing south west wind has shaped them. Continue along the coastal path, resisting the temptation to head for the Shell Beach. As you approach the North Beach you will find Lesser Calamint growing at the edges of the path. Pinch a leaf and smell your fingers. Viper's Bugloss grows in sandy patches here too. The big tough grass is Marram.

Turn right and head across the common towards Shell Beach. You will need to get down on your hands and knees and crawl about in the short turf to find the tiny specialities Fairy Flax, Wild Thyme, Salad Burnet and of course Daisy which looks daintier, pinker and prettier here. The very prickly Burnet Rose grows all over the common. Early summer is the time to appreciate its sheer beauty. If you visit later in the year you will see its round red fruits.

When you arrive at Shell Beach you will see a half-buried fence and great plants of New Zealand Flax both put there to stop erosion. They are doing their job. The new dunes at the top of the beach are being colonised naturally by plants. Their long roots hold the sand together. The grass is Sand Sedge and amongst it grows Sea Holly, Rest Harrow and Common Bird's Foot Trefoil. One wonders how they ever find enough water to survive.

The path now continues past the kiosk and takes the traveller along the cliff edge right round to the harbour. May is the best month for flowers. There are Bluebells, Foxgloves, Sea Campion, Red Campion, Nottingham Catchfly (not found in Guernsey) and all the other botanical friends you have already met on the cliffs in Guernsey.

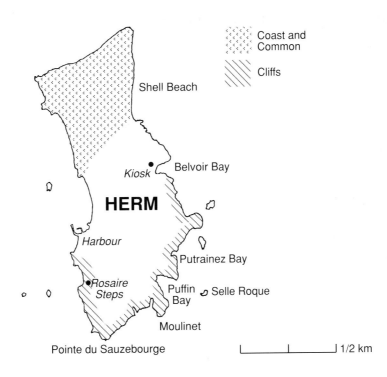

Coast and
Common

Cliffs

Shell Beach

Kiosk ● Belvoir Bay

HERM

Harbour

Putrainez Bay

●Rosaire
Steps

Puffin
Bay ↝ Selle Roque

Moulinet

Pointe du Sauzebourge

⊢————⊣————⊣ 1/2 km

CLIFFS AND CLIFF VALLEYS
Plate 1

GLADDON. Iris foetidissima.

Often called Stinking Iris. Flowers mauve with brown veins. Plants up to 60cm, with red berries in the autumn. In shade and in the open. Flowers June to July. A+, S+, H+.

GREATER BROOMRAPE. Orobanche rapum-genistae.

Tall, stiff, yellowish-brown leafless plant to 40cm. Flowers in spikes. June to August. Parasitic on broom and rarely on gorse. A+, S-, H-.

THRIFT. Armeria maritima.

Rounded pink flower heads on stalks up to 18cm. Leaves small and narrow, forming large clumps. Flowers April to July, all round the coast. A+, S+, H+.

SEA CAMPION. Silene maritima.

Flowers swollen below swelling with pink veins. Petals white. Stems to 15cm, little or not branched. Flowering May to August. A+, S+, H+.

NOTTINGHAM CATCHFLY. Silene nutans.

A tufted plant up to 60cm with narrow, downy leaves. Yellow-white petals rolled back in older flowers. May to August. Common in Herm, not found in Guernsey. A+, S-, H+.

SHAGGY MOUSE-EAR HAWKWEED. Pilosella peleterana.

Yellow dandelion flowers with thicker stems and leaves with many shaggy hairs, whitish underneath and short runners up-turned at the tip. Up to 15cm, flowering May to September. A+, S+, H+.

GOLDEN SAMPHIRE. Inula crithmoides.

Thick fleshy leaves, low on cliffs. Yellow daisy-like flowers from July to October. A+, S+, H-.

SEA PLANTAIN. Plantago maritima.

Leaves fleshy, long and narrow, untoothed. Flowers form an erect green spike up to 20cm tall. The more common Ribwort Plantain (P. lanceolata), has rough wrinkled leaves. Flowers June to August. A-, S+, H-.

BUCKS-HORN PLANTAIN. Plantago coronopus.

Leaves deeply toothed, downy. Flower spikes curving upwards. Locally abundant and variable in size. Flowers May to July. A+, S+, H+.

PORTLAND SPURGE. Euphorbia portlandica.

Low spreading plant with grey-green leaves mostly up the stem, contrasting with the red stalks. Flowers greenish yellow, May to September. A+, S+, H+.

CLIFFS AND CLIFF VALLEYS
Plate 2

FOXGLOVE. Digitalis purpurea.

Tall spikes of long tubular pinkish-purple flowers spotted within. Plants up to 2m. Basal leaves large, downy and wrinkled. Flowers May to July. A+, S+, H+.

BROOM. Cytisus scoparius.

Dark green stems up to 2m with very small leaves. Yellow flowers from May to July. Cliffs and coasts, not nearly as common as Gorse. Grows absolutely prostrate on the cliffs of Alderney, and in Guernsey at Pleinmont. A+, S+, H+.

IVY BROOMRAPE. Orobanche hederae.

Shorter than Greater Broomrape. Flowers usually veined with purple. Parasitic on ivy, so also occurs on walls and banks. Flowers June to August. A+, S+, H+.

BELL HEATHER. Erica cinerea.

Spikes of oval, bright purple flowers at top of woody stems with very narrow evergreen leaves. Plants can be prostrate or up to 30cm. Cliffs and commons, not very frequent. May to September. A+, S+, H+.

HARE'SFOOT CLOVER. Trifolium arvense.

Small plant 10-20cm, with pinkish, oval, compact fluffy flowerheads, downy stems and leaves. Flowering June to September. A+, S+, H+.

OX-EYE DAISY. Leucanthemum vulgare.

Large white daisy flowers from May to September. Leaves toothed, upper ones clasping stem. Plants reach 50cm, often shorter in poor soil. A+, S+, H+.

COMMON KNAPWEED. Centaurea nigra.

Purple flower heads with brown bristly base. Flowering June to September. Plants to 40cm. Also in hedges and on waste ground. A+, S+, H-.

SAND CROCUS. Romulea columnae.

A tiny mauve crocus to 10cm high. Flowers open best in full sun, April. Leaves narrow and curly. Found on cliffs and sandy short turf near the sea, locally plentiful. A+, S+, H+.

COMMON DODDER. Cuscuta epithymum.

A parasite on gorse, also on other plants in turf, with red twining stems and stalkless bunches of waxy white-pink flowers. Stems often dense and tangled. Flowers June to September. A+, S+, H+.

GORSE. Ulex europaeus.

The very spiny dense bushes cover large areas of common and cliffs, with strongly scented dark yellow flowers in most months. Can grow to 1-2m. A+, S+, H+.

BUTCHER'S BROOM. Ruscus aculeatus.

Very stiff evergreen stems up to 75cm. Tiny greenish flowers sit on what look like leaves but are in fact modified stems. Flowers March to April. Red-berried fruit not common. A+, S+, H+.

CLIFFS AND CLIFF VALLEYS
Plate 3

GIANT RHUBARB. Gunnera tinctoria.

Huge leaves up to 2m across, prickly stems. Flowers minute in dense cone shaped spikes. Originally planted, but seeds itself by streams. Flowers May to June. A-, S+, H-.

GOLDEN SAXIFRAGE. Chrysoplenium oppositifolium.

Plants up to 15cm with flat, golden yellow flower heads, April to August. On sides of shady streams or very close to them. A-, S-, H-.

BOREAU'S FUMITORY. Fumaria muralis, sps boraei.

Leaves smoky grey-green and finely divided. Flowers in small spikes, each flower pink with purple tips seen in most months of the year. Also on banks and wasteland. A+, S+, H+.

BLUEBELL. Hyacinthoides non-scripta.

Flower spikes up to 40cm with flowers hanging downwards. Frequent on cliffs, banks and under trees. Flowering May to June. A+, S+, H+.

EARLY SCURVY-GRASS. Cochlearia danica.

A prostrate plant occurring in sandy areas. Leaves stalked and many ivy-shaped. Flowers lilac from February to September. A+, S+, H+.

RED CAMPION. Silene dioica.

Flowers pink, found in most months. Plant reaches 50cm. Plentiful on cliff paths and on hedges, banks and other places. A+, S+, H+.

COMMON DOG VIOLET. Viola riviniana.

Small tufted plant up to 15cm with scentless blue-violet flowers, March to April. Also in hedgebanks and gardens in most areas. A+, S+, H+.

HERB BENNET. Geum urbanum.

Small yellow flowers on plants up to 50cm tall, flowering in May to September. Seed head with small brown hooks. In damp valleys on cliffs, occasional in other habitats. A+, S+, H-.

PRIMROSE. Primula vulgaris.

Pale yellow flowers with darker yellow centre. Leaves light green and wrinkled. As well as cliffs, common on banks throughout the islands. Flowers February to May. A+, S+, H+.

COASTS AND COMMONS
Plate 4

SEA RADISH. Raphanus maritimus.

Large plant up to 1.5m high, very common around the coast, with small yellow or white four-petalled flowers from May to September. A+, S-, H+.

YELLOW HORNED POPPY. Glaucium flavum.

Large yellow flowers from June to September. Distinctive long curved seed-pod up to 25 cm. On shingle banks. A+, S-, H+.

KAFFIR FIG. Carpobrotus edulis.

Sometimes called the Hottentot Fig. Dark green fleshy leaves. It can cover large areas, but is killed off by heavy frost. Pink or yellow flowers up to 5cm across. Occurs June to September. A-, S-, H-.

SEA ROCKET. Cakile maritima.

Quite rare, at top of beaches in sand. Sprawling stems with fleshy leaves and pale mauve flowers from June to September. A+, S-, H+.

SEA SANDWORT. Honkenya peploides.

Creeping plant in sand or shingle at top of beaches. Shiny green fleshy leaves and small white flowers from May to August. A+, S-, H-.

SEA STOCK. Matthiola incana.

Large plants up to 60cm high with mauve scented flowers 3mm across from May to September. A+, S-, H-.

SMALL FLOWERED CATCHFLY. Silene gallica.

Spikes of small flowers, which occur in three colour forms - pale pink, rose pink and those with a dark crimson spot on each petal. Flowers May to August. A+, S+, H+.

PALE FLAX. Linum bienne.

Found in grassy areas. Slender somewhat inconspicuous plant up to 30cm with small narrow leaves and pale blue, short-lived flowers from May to August. A+, S+, H-

SEA KALE. Crambe maritima.

Large clumps of tough, greyish, hairless leaves with dome shaped heads of small white flowers from June to September. At top of beach or sand or shingle. Rare. A+, S-, H-.

FROSTED ORACHE. Atriplex laciniata.

Sprawling plant at top of beaches with grey frosted leaves and pink stems. Flowers small and inconspicuous from June to September. A+, S-, H-.

TREE MALLOW. Lavatera arborea.

Woody stems up to 2m, with soft downy leaves and large dark pink flowers from May to September. A+, S+, H+.

COASTS AND COMMONS
Plate 5

FRAGRANT EVENING PRIMROSE. Oenothera stricta.

Large fragrant yellow flowers, fading to orange from June to September. Plants up to 50cm. Not common. One or two rather similar kinds occur where flowers do not fade to orange. A+, S-, H+.

BURNET ROSE. Rosa pimpinellifolia.

Mostly on the commons. Plants from 5-50cm, stems covered in short, dense prickles. Flowers cream, sometimes pink, followed by black globular fruit. Flowers May to July. A+, S+, H+.

SEA HOLLY. Eryngium maritimum.

Blue-grey spiky leaves and bluish globular flower heads from June to September. The well branched plant grows to about 40cm. Rare in sand dunes . A+, S-, H+.

TREE LUPIN. Lupinus arboreus.

Plants up to 1.5m with spikes of pale yellow flowers often tinged mauve. On sandy soils. Flowers May to August. A+, S+, H+.

MUSK THISTLE. Carduus nutans.

Flower heads large, rounded, rich purplish red and drooping. May to August. Not common. A+, S-, H-.

COCK'S-EGGS. Salpichroa origanifolia.

Large sprawling plant with small white flowers hanging downwards, followed by whitish berries. Leaves small. Flowers May to June. A-. S-, H-.

DUKE OF ARGYLL'S TEA TREE. Lycium barbarum.

Shrub with long, arching, sometimes spiny stems up to 1m high. Small purple flowers followed by red berries, May to September. A+, S-, H-.

MARRAM. Ammophila arenaria.

A creeping perennial of the grass family with stiff sharp-pointed leaves. Flower-heads long, whitish and shaped like a fox's brush. July to August. A+, S-, H+.

COASTS AND COMMONS
Plate 6

AUTUMN LADY'S TRESSES. Spiranthes spiralis.

Small spikes of fragrant white flowers arranged spirally arise from a rosette of leaves. Flowering August to September in short turf, including lawns. A+, S+, H-.

LOUSEWORT. Pedicularis sylvatica.

Often on land that is damp in winter. Pink flowers April to September. Leaves often bronze tinted. A+, S+, H-.

ROSY GARLIC. Allium roseum.

Flower heads with pink flowers and red bulbils, narrow green leaves and stems 40cm, in sandy places. Flowers May to June. A-, S-, H-.

RED BARTSIA. Odontites veruo.

Rather stiff spikes of small pink flowers. Whole plant often purplish, up to 30cm. Flowers July to September. A+, S-, H-.

SHARP RUSH. Juncus acutus.

Stout, erect clumps of very stiff, sharply pointed leaves up to 1m tall. Flowers in dark roundish heads, May to August. A+, S-, H+.

COMMON CENTAURY. Centaurium erythraea.

Small pink flowers in clusters on stems between 5-20cm from May to September, mainly around the coasts. A+, S+, H+.

SALAD BURNET. Sanguisorba minor.

Grey green leaves divided into paired and toothed leaflets. Rounded reddish flower heads at the top of long stalks, May to September. Whole plant up to 30cm. A+, S-, H+.

FAIRY FLAX. Linum catharticum.

Erect, delicate plant with little white flowers and narrow leaves, May to August. 5-15cm high. Found in short turf. A+, S-, H+.

AUTUMN SQUILL. Scilla autumnalis.

Small flower spike with purplish blue flowers appearing before narrow, fleshy, curled leaves. Up to 12cm. Flowers July to October. A+, S+, H+.

VIPER'S BUGLOSS. Echium vulgare.

Stiff blue and purple flower spikes to 60m, June to August. Whole plant covered with short bristles. Very rare in Guernsey, frequent in Herm. A+, S+, H+.

DAISY. Bellis perennis.

Abundant and familiar in grassy places in all the islands. Stems up to 10cm and flowers white to pink especially at back of petals. March to November. A+, S+, H+.

HEATH GROUNDSEL. Senecio sylvaticus.

Whole plant grey and downy, up to 45cm with small yellow flowers from June to September. Also occurs on cliffs. A+, S+, H+.

DOVESFOOT CRANESBILL. Geranium molle.

A low often prostrate loosely haired annual, 12-20 cm high with flowers pinkish purple. Leaves rounded and lobed. Flowers April to September. A+, S+, H+.

COASTS AND COMMONS
Plate 7

SLENDER THISTLE. Carduus tenuiflorus.

Small pink flowers in narrow heads and greyish leaves. Grows in sandy places in clumps up to 60cm. Flowers May to August. A+, S+, H+.

CARROT. Daucus carota.

Rough stemmed plants up to 50cm with feathery leaves and broad white flower heads. Central flower often dull crimson, June to September. A+, S+, H+.

BLACKBERRY. Rubus fructicosus.

Long straggling stems with curved spines forming thick bushes. Common in many areas. White or pink flowers from May to August followed by the well known black berries. A+, S+, H+.

SMALL-FLOWERED MELILOT. Melilotus indica.

Small, narrow heads of tiny deep yellow flowers with hairless trefoil leaves, June to September. Grows to 30cm. Not common. A+, S-, H-.

COMMON CHAMOMILE. Chamaemelum nobile.

Daisy-like flowers from May to September. Leaves feathery and fragrant when crushed. Plants usually 10cm high. A+, S+, H-.

SELF-HEAL. Prunella vulgaris.

Squarish purple flower heads, with pairs of leaves on stem up to 20cm. Flowers June to September. A+, S+, H+.

CLARY. Salvia verbenaca.

Spikes of mauvish blue flowers up to 50cm tall from June to September. Leaves wrinkled. A+, S-, H+.

COASTS AND COMMONS
Plate 8

AT TOP OF PLATE

SAND SPURREY. Spergularia rubra.

Low, spreading plant with slightly sticky stems. Flowers pale pink with undivided petals. May to September. A+, S+, H-.

CREEPING CINQUEFOIL. Potentilla reptans.

Stems creep along ground and root. Leaves with 5-7 leaflets. Yellow flowers on long stalks. May to September. A+, S+, H+.

LADY'S BEDSTRAW. Galium verum.

Typically creeping, low plant in short turf. Can be found taller elsewhere (up to 30cm). Bright yellow flowers from June to September. A+, S+, H+.

SEA BINDWEED. Calystegia soldanella.

Flowers pink with white stripes, 4cm across, June to September. Leaves small, kidney shaped and fleshy. Plant creeping in sand dunes. A+, S-, H+.

AT BOTTOM OF PLATE

KIDNEY VETCH. Anthyllis vulneraria.

Very rare on Guernsey cliffs. Less rare in Alderney and Sark. Flowers orange, yellow or red in crowded head. Leaves and stems downy, spreading up to 20cm. Flowers May to July. A+, S+, H-.

WALL-PEPPER. Sedum acre.

A typical stonecrop with numerous fat yellow-green leaves and yellow star-like flowers. June to July. A+, S-, H+.

CHANGING FORGET-ME-NOT. Myosotis discolor.

Flower heads start curled, the tiny flowers opening pale creamy yellow then changing to grey blue. Stems 5-15cm sprawling. May to June. A+, S+, H+.

ENGLISH STONECROP. Sedum anglicum.

Small fleshy plants often tinged red, up to 4cm high, with starry white flowers from June to September, in sandy soils. A+, S+, H+.

REST-HARROW. Ononis repens.

A low, creeping plant found on commons and hedge banks. Dark green, sticky hairy leaves. Pink flowers from June to September. A+, S+, H+.

SWEET ALISON. Lobularia maritima.

Small sprawling plants to 15cm with rounded white flower heads with sweet scent. In flower most of the year in poor sandy soil. A+, S+, H+.

COMMON BIRD'S-FOOT TREFOIL. Lotus corniculatus.

Common in short turf all over the island. Red buds followed by yellow flowers then brown seed-pods shaped like a bird's foot. Flowers May to September. A+, S+, H+.

WILD THYME. Thymus praecox.

Forming mats of dark green in short turf. Leaves aromatic. Small heads of pink flowers June to September. A+, S+, H+.

EYEBRIGHT. Euphrasia officinalis.

Stiff spikes of tiny white, mauve veined flowers with small dark green, often bronzy leaves 2-12cm. Flowers June to September. A+, S+, H+.

WALLS AND BANKS
Plate 9

RED VALERIAN. Centranthus ruber.

Grey-green hairless leaves and oval flower heads of dark pink, pale pink or white. May to September. Plant up to 45cm. A+, S+, H+.

PINK OXALIS. Oxalis articulata.

Pale green trefoil leaves. Plants can reach 20cm, very pale mauve pink flowers, April to October. Needs some degree of shade. A+, S+, H+.

BEAKED HAWKSBEARD. Crepis vesicaria.

An erect plant 20-50cm high with strong reddish stems. Yellow flower heads 2cm across with outer petals orange underneath. Flowers May to June. A+, S+, H-.

PELLITORY. Parietaria judaica.

Grey-green leaves, hairy and slightly sticky with tiny greenish-red flowers in bunches on pink stems to 50cm high. Flowers June to September. A+, S+, H+.

ST PETER PORT DAISY. Erigeron mucronatus.

Daisy-like flowers with narrow petals, fading pink. Plants up to 30cm on walls mainly in Town. Flowers April to October. A-, S+, H-.

HERB ROBERT. Geranium robertianum.

Plants 50-60cm, often tinged red, leaves deeply dissected. Flowers pink, April to September. A+, S+, H-.

SHEEPS-BIT.   Jasione montana.

Looks rather like small scabius. Narrow leaves. Flowers in a rounded head soft blue. May onwards. A+, S+, H+.

IVY-LEAVED TOADFLAX. Cymbalaria muralis.

Plant trailing down walls, leaves small, ivy shaped. Flowers small, mauve, April to November. A+, S+, H+.

WALL PENNYWORT. Umbilicus rupestris.

Very common especially on walls and banks. Disc-like leaves with spikes of green-brown flowers of varying height up to 30cm. June to August. A+, S+, H+.

WOOD SAGE. Teucrium scorodonia.

Greenish-yellow flowers in pairs on stalks up to 30cm. Oval leaves somewhat downy. July to September. A+, S+, H+.

WALLS AND BANKS
Plate 10

BALM-LEAVED FIGWORT. Scrophularia scorodonia.

> Flowering stem branched. Small brownish flowers June to September. Stalks square, leaves wrinkled, heart shaped. Plant up to 1m. A-, S-, H+.

ALEXANDERS. Smyrnium olustratum.

> Shiny, bright green leaves and yellow green flower heads, on large plants up to 1.5m tall. Flowering March to August. Common also on cliffs and wasteland. A+, S+, H+.

PURPLE TOADFLAX. Linaria purpurea.

> Tall spikes of purple flowers up to 50cm. June to August. Leaves small and narrow. A-, S+, H-.

LESSER CALAMINT. Calamintha nepeta.

> Grey green downy aromatic leaves on stems to 60cm. Flowers mauve-blue in spikes, May to September. Rather rare in Guernsey. A-, S-, H+.

BIRD'S-EYE SPEEDWELL. Veronica chamaedrys.

> Spikes of bright blue flowers, 1-3 flowers open at a time. Stems up to 20cm. April to August. Leaves clasping stem, toothed and downy. A+, S+, H+.

STINKING ONIONS. Allium triquetrum.

> Bundles of white bell-shaped flowers with narrow green stripes hanging from top of three-cornered stem to 25cm. Leaves long and narrow, smelling of garlic. Common in most areas, especially bases of hedge banks. May to June. A+, S+, H+.

HEDGE BEDSTRAW. Galium mollugo .

> Floppy scrambling plant. Flowers small, white in much branched spreading terminal clusters. July to August. A+, S+, H+.

HEDGE WOUNDWORT. Stachys sylvatica.

Widespread on banks. Plant 30-40cm. Flower spikes with crimson purple flowers with white spots. Leaves and stems with rough bristles. Strong smell when rubbed. Flowers June to September. A+, S+, H-.

HEMP AGRIMONY. Eupatorium cannabinum.

Large plant up to 1.25m with dusty pink flowerheads from July to September. Stems pinkish, leaves fingered and toothed. A-, S+, H-.

WET MEADOWS
Plate 11

REED. Phragmites australis.

Very common in marshy areas and occasionally elsewhere. Plants can reach 3m, often shorter. Stems and leaves tough, used for thatching. Flowers a loose feathery purplish spike, August to October. A+, S+, H+.

YELLOW IRIS. Iris pseudacorus.

Distinctive tall plants up to 1.5m, with stiff, long, narrow leaves and yellow iris flowers 2-4 per stem. June to August. A+, S+, H+.

GREAT REED-MACE. Typha latifolia.

In wet places including water filled quarries. Distinctive velvety brown flower spike and tall narrow leaves, up to 2.5m tall. Flowers June to August. A+, S-, H-

HEMLOCK WATER DROPWORT. Oenanthe crocata.

Large plant up to 2m high, flat flower heads of white flowers, June to August. Leaves bright green, hairless, divided into smaller leaflets. Very poisonous, thus removed by farmers. A-, S+, H+.

WATER MINT. Mentha aquatica.

Quite common in damp places. Plants up to 30cm, with green leaves often tinged purple and small, pale mauve, roundish flower heads, July to September. Covered in downy hairs and pleasantly aromatic when bruised. A+, S+, H+.

YELLOW BARTSIA. Parentucellia viscosa.

In several places as well as wet habitats but not common. Stiff spikes of pale yellow flowers, and small green toothed leaves covered in sticky hairs. Flowers June to September. A+, S+, H–.

WET MEADOWS
Plate 12

LESSER SPEARWORT. Ranunculus flammula.

Plant up to 40cm, often smaller, branched hairless stems often reddish at base. Flower a small buttercup, June to October. A+, S+, H+.

SOUTHERN MARSH ORCHID. Dactylorhiza praetermissa.

Slightly larger than the spotted orchids. Flowers usually darker pink and leaves not spotted. Up to 50cm. May to July. A+, S-, H-.

RAGGED ROBIN. Lychnis flos-cuculi.

Delicately cut pink petals, seen May to August, occasionally white flowers seen. Plant reaches 50c, only in damp places. A+, S-, H-.

LOOSE-FLOWERED ORCHID. Orchis laxiflora.

Spikes of rich purple flowers up to 50cm tall. Occasionally pink or white flowered plants also seen. May to July. Leaves narrow and not spotted. A-, S-, H-

MEADOW BUTTERCUP. Ranunculus acris.

Tall buttercup, to 60cm, with well cut leaves, flowering in April to October. Mainly in damp meadows. A+, S+, H+.

HEATH SPOTTED ORCHID. Dactylorhiza maculata.

Not always easy to tell from Common-spotted, but markings on flower usually less clear, paler and lower edge of petals frilly and less toothed. Leaves spotted. May to July. A-, S+, H+.

AMPHIBIOUS BISTORT. Polygonum amphibium.

Creeping on mud, or with roots submerged and leaves floating on surface of water. Flowers small and pink in a dense spike, June to September. A+, S-, H-.

COMMON SPOTTED ORCHID. Dactylorhiza fuchsii.

Flowers pink or white with darker markings, dots and lines. Forms a flower spike up to 45cm. May to July. Leaves with dark spots. A+, S-, H-.

TUFTED WATER FORGET-ME-NOT. Myosotis laxa.

Always in damp habitats. Flowers small and bright blue. Leaves small and narrow with fine hairs. Flowers May to August. A-, S-, H-.

WASTELAND, GARDENS AND FARMLAND
Plate 13

COW PARSLEY. Anthriscus sylvestris.

Plants up to 85cm high, leaves finely cut. Flat round flower heads of small white flowers. Very rare in Guernsey although quite common in Alderney and on mainland. Flowers April to June. A+, S-, H-.

BLACK HOREHOUND. Ballota nigra.

Erect stems, often dusty looking, with dull green rough leaves, and whorls of small purple flowers. Smells strongly when crushed. Flowers June to September. A+, S+, H+.

SCENTLESS MAYWEED. Tripleurospermum inodorum.

Large daisy-like flowers on reddish sprawling stems, with feathery green leaves. Flowers May to September. Also common round coast. A+, S+, H+.

RAGWORT. Senecio jacobaea.

Bright yellow flowers in loose clusters from May to September. Common in many places. Up to 1.5m high. A+, S+, H+.

MUGWORT. Artemesia vulgaris.

Plant up to 1m, with regularly cut leaves, dark green above, silvery beneath. Flowers in small spikes, inconspicuous, June to September. A+, S-, H+.

BRISTLY OXTONGUE. Picris echioides.

Sharp bristles all over the plant, with large white ones studding leaves. Up to 1m tall, with yellow flowers, June to September. A+, S+, H-.

KEELED CORNSALAD. Valerianella carinata.

Small creeping plant, also on walls and banks. Untoothed green leaves and very small light blue flowers, April to August. A+, S+, H+.

GLADIOLUS. Gladiolus byzantinus.

Large spikes of magenta flowers, up to 70cm tall, June to August. Seen here and there, never in large numbers. Used to be cultivated. A+, S+, H+.

CORN MARIGOLD. Chrysanthemum segetum.

Golden yellow daisy flowers, May to September. Leaves and stems grey-green and hairless. Up to 35cm. A+, S+, H+.

YARROW. Achillea millefolium.

Plants up to 30cm, leaves small, dark green and feathery. Flower heads round and flat, white to pink, May to September. A+, S+, H+.

WASTELAND, GARDENS AND FARMLAND
Plate 14

GIANT ECHIUM. Echium pininana.

A garden escape. Basal rosette of large leaves. Flower spike up to 4m tall with small blue flowers, May to September. A+, S+, H+.

HOGWEED. Heracleum sphondylium.

Large flat heads of white flowers, the outermost with larger outer petals. Leaves and stems very rough, up to 2.5m. Flowers April to November. A+, S+, H+.

FENNEL. Foeniculum vulgare.

Feathery leaves, smell strongly when crushed. Plant can reach 2.5m. Yellow flat flower heads, May to September. A+, S+, H+.

GREAT WILLOW-HERB. Epilobium hirsutum.

Tall plant up to 2m. Leaves and stems downy. Purple-pink flowers about 2cm across, June to September. Also in damp areas. A+, S-, H+.

COMMON MALLOW. Malva sylvestris.

Leaves large, rounded. Flowers mauve pink with darker lines, May to September. Plant reaches 1m. A+, S+, H+.

GUERNSEY COLTSFOOT. Petasites fragrans.

Large rounded leaves on short stalks. Flower heads a loose bunch of pinkish purple flowers, faintly fragrant. December to March. A+, S+, H+.

GUERNSEY FLEABANE. Conyza sumatrensis.

A common weed in autumn. Plant can reach 1.5m high. Flowers inconspicuous, small and whitish. Leaves narrow and green. A-, S-, H-.

WASTELAND, GARDENS AND FARMLAND
Plate 15

BLADDER CAMPION. Silene vulgaris.

A greyish-green, usually hairless plant 20-60cm high. Leaves oval and pointed. Flowers white with five petals. May to August. A+, S-, H-.

CAPE CUDWEED. Gnaphalium undulatum.

Stems reach 75cm. Leaves green above but covered with thick white hairs below, as is the rest of the plant. Flowers small golden bunches, May to September. A+, S+, H+.

SAND SEDGE. Carex arenaria.

Stems creep along sandy soil rooting for many metres. Flower stalks reach about 60cm but often shorter. A+, S-, H+.

BLACK NIGHTSHADE. Solanum nigrum.

A common weed up to 30cm, dull green leaves, small white flowers produce green round berries which turn black. Flowers May to September. A+, S+, H+.

AMERICAN BELLBINE. Calystegia silvatica.

Flowers large, white and trumpet shaped, about 6cm across, May to September. Leaves arrow-head shaped, stems thin, creeping or climbing up to 2-3m long. A+, S+, H-

BORAGE. Borago officinalis.

Often grown as a culinary herb, grows wild in scattered places. Plant up to 50cm covered in short prickly hairs. Flowers bright blue with white centre and purple-black stamens. Flowers April to November. A+, S+, H-.

MEXICAN OXALIS. Oxalis latifolia.

Three leaflets at end of juicy stems with small orange spots beneath. Five-petalled pink flowers appear April to October. Up to 30cm tall. A+, S+, H+.

LESSER CELANDINE. Ranunculus ficaria.

Plant up to 20cm. Shiny green heart shaped leaves and bright yellow flowers. Back of petals bronze. Flowers February to May. A+, S+, H+.

IVY. Hedera helix.

Common in most areas, crawling and climbing over banks, walls, trees etc. Leaves dark, shiny green, flowers pale green in round heads. September to December followed by black berries. A+, S+, H+.

BITTERSWEET. Solanum dulcamara.

Often climbing in hedges, stems up to 1.5m long. Small purple flowers followed by yellow oval berries ripening to red. Flowers May to September. A+, S+, H+.

WASTELAND, GARDENS AND FARMLAND
Plate 16

HONEYSUCKLE. Lonicera periclymenum.

A climber with opposite oval leaves. Flowers cream deepening to orange-buff, tinged red outside and sweet scented. June to September. A+, S+, H+.

DANDELION. Taraxacum officinalis.

Golden yellow flowers. Flower stalk leafless, hollow, with staining white juice. Leaves deeply toothed, hairless. Common also on cliffs in turf. Flowers April to October. A+, S+, H+.

RED CLOVER. Trifolium pratense.

Trefoil leaves, downy on 20-30cm stems. Dark pink flowers in globular heads from May to October. A+, S+, H+.

WHITE CLOVER. Trifolium repens.

Smaller plant than Red Clover creeping to 20cm, leaflets hairless. Rounded white flower heads with dead brown flowers beneath. Flowers May to October. A+, S+, H+.

COMMON CAT'S-EAR. Hypochaeris radicata.

Yellow dandelion-like flower heads, one on each stalk, tiny leaflets on stalks. Leaves narrow toothed and bristly, forming a basal rosette. Flowering June to September. A+, S+, H+.

TORMENTIL. Potentilla erecta.

Slender and often prostrate with thread-like stems. Leaves nearly always three-toothed. Flowers rather like small buttercups. May onwards. A+, S+, H+.

SMOOTH SOW THISTLE. Sonchus oleraceus.

A greyish, hairless plant stem 15cm-1m high with milky sap and hollow stems. Slightly prickly leaves. Flowerheads in clusters and yellow. Flowers May onwards. A+, S+, H+.

NEAPOLITAN GARLIC. Allium neapolitanum.

Small white flowers, erect in heads at top of weak flower stems up to 50cm high. Leaves long and narrow. Flowers May to June. Known in Guernsey as Star of Bethlehem. A-, S-, H-.

COMMON POPPY. Papaver rhoeas.

Large flowers with scarlet petals blotched black at base. Stems up to 55cm, June to October. Leaves very divided and hairy. A+, S+, H+.

WILD LEEK. Allium ampeloprasum.

Rounded stalks up to 2m, with large round flower heads of pinkish flowers about 8cm in diameter. Leaves long, smelling of garlic, withering at flowering time. Mainly near coasts and wasteland. Flowers June to August. A-, S-, H+.

REFERENCE BOOKS

For those people who have become interested in wild flowers and wish to carry their studies further, there are a number of colour illustrated guides. These are listed below and should be obtainable from most book shops.

A FIELD GUIDE TO THE WILD FLOWERS OF BRITAIN AND NORTHERN EUROPE by David Sutton.

GUIDE TO THE WILD FLOWERS OF THE BRITISH ISLES AND NORTHERN EUROPE by Pamela Forey.

In addition to the above there are a number of local botanical books or booklets. They have no colour illustrations.

THE WILD FLOWERS OF GUERNSEY by David McClintock. This is out of print but can be obtained from La Société Guernesiaise, Candie Gardens, St Peter Port, Guernsey. Price £18.00 plus p&p.

SUPPLEMENT TO THE WILD FLOWERS OF GUERNSEY by David McClintock. Obtainable from La Société Guernesiaise, price £4.00 plus p&p.

THE FLORA OF ALDERNEY, a check list with notes by Brian Bonnard. £2.50

THE WILD FLOWERS OF HERM published by La Société Guernesiaise, £2.50.

THE WILD FLOWERS OF SARK.

MAPS

In Guernsey the best maps to use for finding your way about are: PERRY'S GUIDE and the GUERNSEY TOURIST MAP 1: 25,000. This is the nearest you will get to an Ordinance Survey map in Guernsey. The smaller islands do not present such a problem and maps can be bought from suitable shops on all three islands.

COUNTRY CODE

Please:

Respect private property.

Do not enter fields containing cows or horses.

Close all gates.

Do not dig up wild plants it is against the law.

Do not pick any orchids. If you do pick wild flowers be sensible and pick them in small numbers.

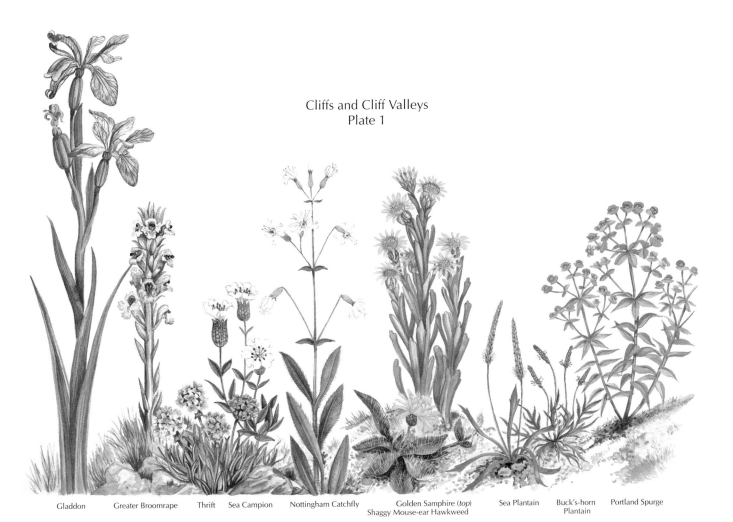

Cliffs and Cliff Valleys
Plate 1

Gladdon   Greater Broomrape   Thrift   Sea Campion   Nottingham Catchfly   Golden Samphire (*top*)   Sea Plantain   Buck's-horn   Portland Spurge
Shaggy Mouse-ear Hawkweed   Plantain

Cliffs and Cliff Valleys
Plate 2

Foxglove   Broom   Ivy Broomrape   Bell Heather   Haresfoot Clover   Ox-eye Daisy   Common Knapweed   Butchers Broom (*top*)
Common Dodder   Gorse
Sand Crocus

Cliffs and Cliff Valleys
Plate 3

Giant Rhubarb   Golden Saxifrage   Boreau's Fumitory   Bluebell (*top*)
Early Scurvy Grass   Red Campion(*top*)
Common Dog Violet   Herb Bennet (*top*)
Primrose

Coasts and Commons
Plate 4

Sea Radish (*top*) Kaffir Fig   Sea Rocket   Sea Sandwort   Sea Stock Small Flowered Catchfly   Pale Flax   Sea Kale   Tree Mallow (*top*)
Yellow Horned Poppy   Frosted Orache

Coasts and Commons
Plate 5

Fragrant Evening Primrose (*top*)
Burnet Rose

Sea Holly

Tree Lupin

Musk Thistle

Cocks Eggs   Marram (*top*)
Duke of Argyll's Tea Tree

Coasts and Commons
Plate 6

Autumn Lady's Tresses   Rosy Garlic   Red Bartsia Sharp Rush   Salad Burnet (*top*)   Autumn Squill (*top*)   Daisy   Heath Groundsel
                      Lousewort   Common Centaury Fairy Flax   Vipers Bugloss   Dovesfoot Cranesbill

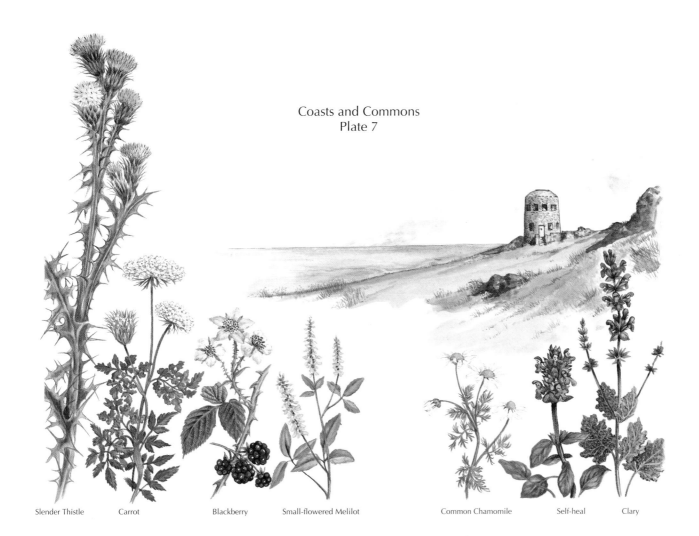

Coasts and Commons
Plate 7

Slender Thistle   Carrot   Blackberry   Small-flowered Melilot   Common Chamomile   Self-heal   Clary

Coasts and Commons
Plate 8

Sand Spurrey (*top*)   Creeping Cinquefoil (*top*)   Lady's Bedstraw (*top*)   Sea Bindweed (*top*)
Kidney Vetch   Changing Forget-me-not   E. Stonecrop   Rest Harrow   Sweet Alison   Common Birds-foot   Wild Thyme   Eyebright
        Wall Pepper (*lower*)   Trefoil

Walls and Banks
Plate 9

Red Valerian (*top*) Beaked Hawks-beard (*top*)
Pink Oxalis Pellitory

St Peter Port Daisy

Herb Robert

Sheeps-bit (*top*)
Ivy-leaved Toadflax

Wood Sage (*top*)
Wall Pennywort

Walls and Banks
Plate 10

Balm-leaved Figwort   Alexanders   Purple Toadflax   Lesser Calamint   Birdseye Speedwell   Stinking Onions   Hedge Woundwort (*top*)   Hemp
                                                                                                                        Hedge Bedstraw   Agrimony

Wet Meadows
Plate 11

Reed   Yellow Iris   Great Reed-Mace   Hemlock Water Dropwort   Water Mint   Yellow Bartsia

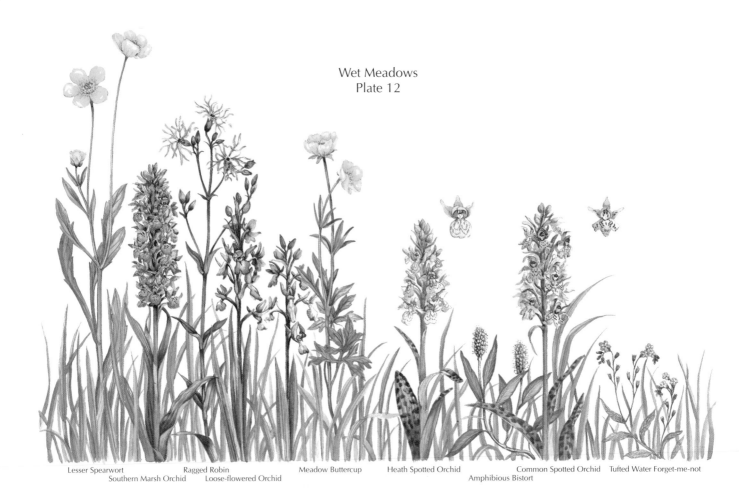

Wet Meadows
Plate 12

Lesser Spearwort

Southern Marsh Orchid

Ragged Robin

Loose-flowered Orchid

Meadow Buttercup

Heath Spotted Orchid

Amphibious Bistort

Common Spotted Orchid

Tufted Water Forget-me-not

Wasteland, Gardens and Farmland
Plate 13

Cow Parsley (*top*)   Scentless   Ragwort   Mugwort   Bristly Oxtongue (*top*)   Gladiolus   Corn Marigold   Yarrow
Black Horewound   Mayweed   Keeled Cornsalad

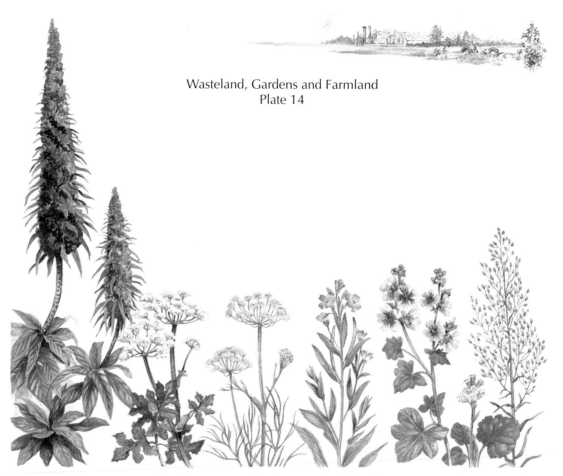

Giant Echium   Hogweed   Fennel   Great Willow-herb   Common Mallow   Guernsey Fleabane (*top*)
                                                                          Guernsey Coltsfoot

Wasteland, Gardens and Farmland
Plate 15

Bladder Campion (*top*)   Sand Sedge   Black Nightshade (*top*)   Borage   Mexican Oxalis   Lesser Celandine   Bittersweet (*top*)
Cape Cudweed   American Bellbine   Ivy

Honeysuckle (*top*)   Red Clover   White Clover Common Cats-ear   Smooth Sow-thistle (*top*)   Common Poppy   Wild Leek
Dandelion   Tormentil   Neapolitan Garlic Barren Strawberry